The [illegible]ale of Jack and the Beanstalk

Written by Tony Bradman
Illustrated by Anna Hopkins

Characters

Jack

Mum

The Giant

Clara the Cow

The Singing Harp

The Hen that Lays Golden Eggs

Scene One

(Jack's house.)

Jack: But **why** do we have to sell Clara, Mum? I don't understand!

Mum: *(Crying)* I've told you, Jack. We used to be rich when you were little and your Dad was alive. Now we need the money – or we'll starve! So off you go to market ... I'll fetch the axe to chop wood for the stove.

(Mum goes out.)

Jack: I wish we weren't poor ... and I wish I could make Mum happy again! But I'm just a boy. What can I do?

Clara: Mooooo ... Not a lot. And if we've got to go, can we get a moooove on?

Jack: Oh, come on then.

(Jack and Clara go out.)

Scene Two

(Jack's house. Jack comes running up to Mum, excited.)

Jack: Look, Mum! I sold Clara ... and this is what I got.

Mum: I don't believe it! You sold our cow for a ... **bean**?

Jack: But it's a **magic** bean, Mum. It might solve all our problems.

Mum: How could you, Jack? We're doomed, doomed!

(Mum runs out, sobbing.)

Jack: Oh no, I've just made things worse! Stupid bean! *(Jack throws the bean out of the window).* Hold on – I think it's sprouting! And now it's growing and growing and growing ... Wow! I wonder what's at the top?

(Jack climbs the beanstalk.)

Scene Three

(The castle at the top of the beanstalk.)

Jack: Phew, that was a hard climb! Hey, what's this? Giant walls, a giant door ... it must be a giant's castle! I'll sneak a peek inside.

(Jack tiptoes in.)

The Giant: *(Heard but not seen)* Fee, fi, fo fum,
I smell the blood of a little one.

Jack: Yikes! He's between me and the door!
I'd better hide.

The Giant: *(Entering and looking around)* Grrr ... nobody here. Shame. I could do with a little one ... on toast. I know. I'll count my lovely gold. Then I'll go and find somebody to eat. I'm **so** wicked, ha ha! One, two, er ... what comes next? Seven, er, four ...

Jack: *(Whispering)* It's not fair! A nasty old giant like him doesn't deserve to be rich.

The Giant: Umm ... counting makes my brain hurt. I need a nap. *(Snores.)*

Jack: *(Whispering)* And we need some of your gold. This bag will do nicely!

(Jack dashes off with his loot.)

Scene Four

(Jack's house.)

Jack: But Mum, why isn't the gold enough to save us? I don't understand!

Mum: I've told you, Jack. Food costs a lot these days. That bag of gold will only last a week – at the most! What are we going to do when it runs out? We'll starve, that's what!

(Mum goes out.)

Jack: I won't let that happen. This calls for another trip to the Giant's castle.

(Suddenly, Clara enters.)

Jack: Hello, Clara. What are you doing here?

Clara: I couldn't stand it there, so I ran away. I just had to moooove.

Jack: Oh well, it's good to have you back. See you later.

(Jack climbs the beanstalk.)

Scene Five

(Inside the castle at the top of the beanstalk.)

Jack: Phew, the Giant's not here, thank goodness! Hold on a minute ...

The Giant: *(Heard, but not seen)* Fee, fi, fo, fum, make an effort, hen, get it done!

Jack: *(Whispering)* Yikes! He's coming this way. I'd better hide.

(The Giant enters with the Hen that Lays Golden Eggs.)

The Hen: *(To the Giant)* I'm trying, OK? But laying golden eggs isn't easy, you know. It **hurts**.

Jack: *(Whispering)* Wow, a hen like that could solve our money problems ... forever!

The Giant: *(To the Hen)* Grrr ... it'll hurt a lot more if you don't lay an egg soon. Now, I'm off to count my lovely gold again. I'm worried some of it is missing. Just make sure there's a nice surprise for me when I come back – or else.

(The Giant goes out.)

Jack: *(Grabbing the Hen)* He'll get a surprise, all right. No golden egg – and no hen, either!

The Hen: Hey! You've ruffled my feathers!

(Jack dashes off with the Hen.)

Scene Six

(Jack's house.)

Jack: Mum! Look, I've got us a hen that lays golden eggs!

The Hen: Ouch. Do you have to talk about that?

Mum: I don't believe it! Where did you find it, anyway?

The Hen: Actually, he stole me.

Mum: How could you, Jack? I'll bet you stole that bag of gold, too. So now we'll probably be hanged before we have a chance to starve. Either way, we're still doomed, doomed!

(Mum runs out, sobbing.)

Clara: Dear oh dear! Mooooo ... she's in a bad mooood!

Jack: I know. I've just made things even worse! I've got to make Mum happy – but how? Maybe I should try my luck in the Giant's castle one last time.

(Jack climbs the beanstalk.)

Scene Seven

(Inside the castle at the top of the beanstalk.)

Jack:	Phew, that climb doesn't get any easier. Now, what can I find?
The Giant:	*(Heard, but not seen)* Fee, fi, fo, fum, Singing Harp, I'm feeling glum!
Jack:	*(Whispering)* Yikes! Here comes old nasty! I'd better hide.
	(The Giant enters with the Singing Harp.)

The Harp: Oh, very well. I'll sing you a song to cheer you up. If you're happy and you know it, clap your hands ...

Jack: *(Whispering)* I've got to get that harp for my Mum! It's sure to make her smile.

The Giant: *(To the Singing Harp)* Grrr ... that's lovely. I **do** feel a bit more cheerful. But my gold's still missing, and so is my hen. I think I'll have another look for them. Just you keep singing, Harpy. I won't be far away.

(The Giant goes out.)

Jack:	*(Grabbing the Singing Harp)* Come on! You should be singing for someone much nicer!
The Harp:	Help, I'm being harp-napped! Stop, thief!
The Giant:	*(Heard, but not seen)* Grrr ... I'll bet that's who took my gold and my hen!
Jack:	Whoops! Time to go.
	(Jack dashes off with the Singing Harp.)

Scene Eight

(Jack's house.)

Jack: I'm sorry, Mum! I took the bag of gold, the hen and the harp from the giant at the top of the beanstalk. I just wanted you to be happy again, but now we're doomed – and it's all my fault! *(Sobs.)*

Mum: You did all that for me, Jack? What a good boy you are!

The Giant: *(Heard but not seen)* Grrr ... Fee, fi, fo, fum, look out down there, here I come. Be you alive, or be you dead, I'll crush your bones to make my bread!

The Hen: I think he's a bit upset.

The Harp: Can't say I blame him myself.

Clara: Moooove over ... I'm off!

Mum: Hey! That sounds like the nasty giant who stole our money ... and ate your Dad! Now we've got him at our mercy. Here's the axe – get chopping!

Jack: With pleasure, Mum! *(Jack chops down the beanstalk.)* The bigger they are the harder they fall! Tim-BER!

The Giant: Aaaargh ... I knew I should have stayed in bed this morning. *(CRASH!)*

Mum and Jack: *(Dancing and hugging each other)* Three cheers for us, hip, hip, hip HOORAY! We'll live happily ever after, from this day!